Party Appetizers

SMALL BITES, BIG FLAVORS

By Tori Ritchie

Photographs by Victoria Pearson

CHRONICLE BOOKS
SAN FRANCISCO

Text copyright © 2004 by Tori Ritchie
Photographs copyright © 2004 by Victoria Pearson

Library of Congress Cataloging-in-Publication Data:

Ritchie, Tori
   Party appetizers : small bites, big flavors / by Tori
Ritchie.— 1st ed.
       p. cm.
Includes index.

ISBN 0-8118-4292-4
1. Appetizers. I. Title.
TX740.R52 2004
641.8′12—dc22

                    2003021669

Manufactured in China.

Design and typesetting by Carole Goodman,
   Blue Anchor Design

Photographer's assistant: Jon Nakano
Prop stylist: Yolande Yorke-Edgell
Prop stylist's assistant: Jennifer Flanagan
Food stylist: Rori Trovato
Food stylist's assistant: Sarah Copeland

Distributed in Canada by Raincoast Books
9050 Shaughnessy Street
Vancouver, BC V6P 6E5

10 9 8 7 6 5 4 3 2 1

Chronicle Books LLC
85 Second Street
San Francisco, California 94105

www.chroniclebooks.com

Ak-Mak is a registered trademark of Soojian's Inc.,
Baci PERUGINA is a registered trademark of Société
des Produits Nestlé S.A., Best Foods is a registered
trademark of Unilever Bestfoods affiliated companies,
Callebaut is a registered trademark of S.A. JACOBS
Suchard-Cote D'Or N.V., Hellmann's is a registered
trademark of Unilever Bestfoods affiliated companies,
Sunset is a registered trademark of Sunset Publishing
Corporation, Tabasco is a registered trademark of
McIlhenny Co., Technicolor is a registered trademark
of Technicolor, Videocassette, B.V.

ACKNOWLEDGMENTS

To Leslie Jonath. We always said we'd do something together and finally we have. Cheers!

To the rest of the team at Chronicle Books, especially Laurel Mainard for being the world's best follower-througher; Ann Martin Rolke for a thoughtful, thorough edit; Victoria Pearson and her team for making the food look even better in the photos; and Carole Goodman for making the words look even better in the designs.

To my recipe tester, Jill Oringer, for her swift and professional results.

To the tasters: Sue and John Ritchie, Charlotte Ritchie, Mark and Jill Ritchie, The Glenbrook Ladies, Vinnie, Callie, the Snows, the Hoods, Loke and Annette, Pen and Clint, Toni and Donn, Nala Kram, The Woodman, Heidi and Alison at Chronicle Mag., Barry, Carol, and Lena, and to Blaise for o.d.-ing on Mocha Shortbreads. To Jan Stefanki, Callie McLellan IV and Callie McLellan V, Katherine Cobbs, Jean Withers, Bibby Gignilliat, Patricia Wells, and Amanda Haas for contributing recipes and ideas. To Mary Risley for teaching me about gougères, croustades, and all things hors d'oeuvre-y. And especially to Lori, Deke, Ellie, Grace, and Derko Hunter for recipe research and for providing the poolhouse kitchen and garden.

To JR and SR for raising me at cocktail parties.

To Sam for eating everything and never complaining about appetizers for breakfast, lunch, and dinner.

TABLE OF CONTENTS

INTRODUCTION

I WAS RAISED AT COCKTAIL PARTIES. SERIAL SOCIALIZERS, my parents looked for any excuse to have friends over to eat, drink, and laugh. Birthdays, car shows, moon landings, July Fourth, Labor Day, Twelfth Night, you name it. Even Christmas Day wasn't exempt. In fact, that was our biggest cocktail party of the year, although we called it an Open House. It started at noon, ended at nine, and revolved around deviled eggs, Bloody Marys, and Irish Coffee. All four children were expected to invite as many friends as we wanted and to hang with the grown-ups for as long as we cared. Even our Pekinese dog was part of it. Presenting him to an uninitiated guest on a silver salver topped with a dome (he actually fit under the thing) was our standard party gag and it worked every time.

I gave my first party at age fifteen, a sit-down dinner for twenty-two sopho-mores with (virgin) drinks and hors d'oeuvres before. Since then I have given too many to remember. In the '80s, they were Bonfire-of-the-Vanities affairs, with vodka frozen in ice, mini eggs Benedict, entire wheels of hot Brie. In the '90s, I sought my inner Italian, which meant crostini, anything with Gorgonzola and vegetables dipped in olive oil and salt and fabulously called *pinzimonio*. Then the tapas craze hit, and I found a whole new fleet of little dishes.

Now when I have friends over, I *only* serve appetizers since I've converted my dining room to a home office and there's no place to eat with knife and fork. I've found it's my favorite way to entertain because it is so casual and unscripted, and no one gets stuck next to someone they find boring. My parties are relaxed and my friends aren't famous or fancy—they're real people, and I invite them over because I love to be with them, not because I want to impress them with perfection in my food and decor. I hope this book will inspire you to invite the people you love over and give you the wherewithal to enjoy the party as much as they do.

PARTY PLANNING 101

The most important thing to remember is that if you're not having a good time, no one will. That's why the simplest parties are the best. But a simple party still needs a plan. That means choosing recipes that don't all have to be assembled at the last minute, shopping at least one day ahead, and cleaning up several hours before guests arrive so you have time to decompress, primp, and feel totally smooth when the first person walks in the door.

To get started, first decide on the mood of the party: is it dressy or casual, themed or random, daytime or evening, inside or out, big or small? Once you have made those choices, invitations should go out. I recommend at least two weeks in advance (unless it's totally spontaneous) by phone, mail, or Internet (I dread e-mail invitations and never send them, but I accept the inevitable). Now it's time to think about the food.

Choosing the Menu

The recipes in this book are designed to be "bite-size," that is, to be eaten out of hand in one or two bites. It's the most convenient way to eat with cocktails and it minimizes cleanup—no plates, no utensils. The chapters are organized the same way I plan menus: First there are salty, crunchy snacks to scatter around the room and platters of dips, spreads, shellfish, and vegetables to place in central areas where people can gather around them. Then come the sexy, warm foods passed by hand—luscious meats and seafood, savory pastries, and melting cheese canapés—followed by colorful, cool finger foods that can also be passed or strategically placed around a room to let people eat without moving apart. Finally, there's something sweet, perhaps a tiny cookie or candy, to nibble on the way out or to be taken home as a memento.

When creating a menu for your party, the occasion will dictate the types of food you want (substantial holiday foods, luxurious ingredients for a fancy night, light vegetables and seafood for summer afternoons, and so on), but always keep balance in mind. Select a few recipes from each of the chapters, aiming for a mix of meat, seafood, cheese, vegetables, and bread- or pastry-based appetizers. Let the season guide you; grilled apricots are great in summer, roasted root vegetables in winter. Don't forget to contrast colors and textures—avoid all brown or all pale foods; get some green or red (or both) in there; vary smooth dips, coarse toppings, and chunky fillings. Consider the shape of the appetizer, too, mixing round, oblong, and wedge-shaped ones. Variety and appearance are as important as taste when each portion is so small.

How Much per Person?

How much depends on the time of day you are having the party, how long people will be there, and if they are going out to eat afterward. It's always better to have too much than too little, so err on the side of generosity. If you are having just a few friends for drinks before you sit down (or go out) to a substantial meal, offer olives or nuts and one or two other appetizers. If it is a longer predinner or pre-event party, offer four or five different appetizers. If it's a full-blown cocktail buffet, offer six to eight kinds of appetizers.

I bank on each person eating at least two portions of each kind of appetizer. The recipes in this book are scaled accordingly, giving you the yield in portions (or quantity, where relevant) and/or servings, so you can calculate how many batches of the recipe you'll need to feed your number of guests. Most of these recipes easily can be doubled to feed more; however, if the yield is 12 servings and you're only having six people, I recommend you make the full amount rather than halving a recipe, unless it is obvious how to do so—most extras will be consumed anyway.

Make-Ahead Strategy

The other element of menu planning is choosing dishes that can be made ahead. Very few should be fussed with in the last half hour before the party, or you will drive yourself crazy. To help you select recipes from this book that can be made in advance versus those that need last-minute preparation, see the table on page 11.

Shopping

Do the shopping at least the day before, but set aside an hour on the day of the party to run out for anything you forgot (it will happen) or for day-of purchases, like oysters. Read through the recipes completely before making a shopping list; be sure to note quantities of every item. I can't tell you how many times I've been at the store and wondered, did I need twelve apricots, or twenty-four? When you get home, trim the bottom stems of tender, leafy herbs (basil, parsley, cilantro, mint) and stand each bunch in a glass of water, as you would flowers. Refrigerate them with a plastic bag inverted over the top. Make sure you don't pile soft fruits and tomatoes in bowls where the bottom ones can get bruised, and don't pack greens and vegetables in refrigerator drawers where they can get smashed. Spread things out, with room to breathe, so they will look their best for the party.

Presentation

Thankfully, gone are the days of bell pepper bowls and hollowed-out cabbages holding dips. Garnishes should be minimal, edible, and echo what's in the recipe. Most of these recipes are attractive enough to stand alone, but if you like to garnish, use a fresh herb from the ingredient list (thus telegraphing to the eater what the flavor is) or one that complements it. Sturdy herbs like thyme, rosemary, chives, spearmint, and Italian parsley are good choices. (Basil and cilantro tend to droop when left on platters, but are fine for passed hors d'oeuvres. Dill is so strong it should only be used when it is in the recipe.) Unsprayed, nontoxic leaves from trees such as lemon, fig, bay, or laurel, as well as grape leaves, add graphic interest. I prefer flowers (especially scented ones) in vases, not on plates, unless there is a flower in the recipe, such as nasturtiums.

For serving platters and dishes, look around the house with fresh eyes every time you have a party. You'd be amazed what can be pressed into use: cutting boards, trays, clean flower pots and their saucers, ceramic tiles, glasses, vases, even pretty baking dishes. Mix shapes and colors for visual interest. Or make a statement with all white serving dishes, or all black—or all purple! And don't forget cocktail napkins . . . lots of them.

A Word about Ingredients

You'll find the requisite luxury foods in this book: caviar, pâté, shellfish, rack of lamb. Appetizers are a great vehicle for the expensive stuff because you can stretch a small amount a long way—a third of a pound of crab for 12 servings, one ounce of caviar for 24 portions. If you've never cooked with these ingredients before, here's your chance.

Good olive oil is indispensable for good appetizers. The following recipes call for extra-virgin olive oil when its distinctive taste is essential, otherwise pure olive oil is fine. Do not use "light" olive oil, which is basically flavorless. Likewise, use imported Parmigiano-Reggiano when it is specified; otherwise, less expensive Parmesan is fine.

Don't be afraid of store-bought foods. I couldn't throw a party without bottled mayonnaise, canned beans, purchased roasted bell peppers, and tortilla chips, to name a few. But while others are filling their pantries with gourmet pestos, tapenades, and all manner of vegetable spreads, I have yet to find any I like better than the homemade versions I offer here, made freshly and quickly (and far less expensively) in a food processor.

Bread is the best little hors d'oeuvres tray there ever was, so invest in the finest baguettes and loaves you can find for cheese, crostini, and croustades. A bread-based appetizer used to be called a canapé, which means "sofa" in French (which I learned when a friend in Paris offered me her *canapé-lit* and I thought it was something to eat, not something to sleep on). I love to think of my figs and Gorgonzola, my fava beans and ricotta salata, resting on a bread sofa.

A Few Things Nobody Mentions

The issue of breath: loads of garlic and raw onions make lousy companions for one-on-one conversation, so keep those to a minimum. Exploding foods, like whole cherry tomatoes (as opposed to hollowed ones), and anything superhot make for embarrassing moments when you are trying to eat and talk and keep your shirt clean. Overloaded skewers can lead to awkward yanking with your teeth. When you serve food on skewers and picks, stick to bite-size quantities and offer a bowl or small glass as a receptacle for the used skewer. Finally, be sure to clean the bathroom before guests arrive and to put out fresh hand towels. I know, I know . . . it sounds obvious, but trust me, some people forget.

In the End

The people are more important than the food. No matter what you serve, how you decorate, or what you wear, only happy guests make a party worthwhile. I've been to many a better salsa and chips fest than boring cocktail buffets, so remember this when you are stressing over the perfect amount of caviar on your stuffed eggs. Ultimately, you are the most important guest, so treat yourself like one and don't demand more than you can give. And have fun!

MAKE-AHEAD PLANNER

WHEN PLANNING YOUR APPETIZERS MENU, YOU WANT mostly recipes that can be made well in advance, including a few that might need last minute touches, and only a few that need to be prepared entirely just before the party starts. This table will help you make those choices at a glance.

Every recipe in the book is listed here. Those marked "Yes" mean the recipe can be prepared an hour or more in advance (in some cases, up to several days), with minimal last-minute work. Those marked "Partial" mean that some of the recipe can be made at least an hour in advance, plus last-minute cooking or preparation. (See each recipe for details on which elements can be made ahead.) If the recipe is marked "No" it means that everything must be prepared and assembled within about 30 minutes of serving.

RECIPE NAME	MAKE AHEAD: YES	PARTIAL	NO
LARGE PLATTERS AND SMALL BITES			
Curry Cashews	X		
Spiked Olives	X		
Rosemary Almonds	X		
Dilled Green Beans	X		
Warm Green Olives			X
Gorgonzola Bites	X		
Two-Olive Tapenade	X		
Roasted Eggplant Dip with Spiced Pita Crisps	X		
Roasted Tomato Salsa	X		
Texas Caviar	X		
Salumi with Italian Salsa	X		
Oysters with Preserved–Meyer Lemon Mignonette		X	
Roasted Vegetable Platter with Arugula Green Goddess Dip	X		
Goat Cheese with Cumin and Mint	X		
Seasonal Cheese and Fruit			X
WARM FINGER FOODS			
Baby Lamb Chops with Mint-Cilantro Relish		X	
Cornmeal Blini with Smoked Salmon	X		
Tandoori Chicken Spears		X	
Merguez Meatballs with Yogurt Sauce	X		
Chorizo and Potatoes with Romesco		X	
Salt-Roasted Prawns with Lemon Pesto	X		
Wild Mushroom Croustades			X
Tomato-Gruyère Tart Squares	X		
Arancini		X	
Cheddar-Chive Gougères	X		
Warm Dates with Sea Salt and Lime			X
Grilled Apricots with Serrano Ham	X		
Sausage-Stuffed Cremini	X		
Fig and Gorgonzola Crostini with Caramelized Onions		X	
Mystery Tidbits and Hasty Hots			X
COOL FINGER FOODS			
Baby Artichokes with Lemon Mayonnaise	X		
Stuffed Eggs Caviar-Style	X		
Parmesan-Pepper Twists	X		
Cured Salmon with Pimentón	X		
Filet Mignon with Horseradish Cream			X
Tuna Poke in Wonton Cups		X	
Foie Gras Pâté on Brioche with Fig Jam	X		
Endive with Crab Salad			X
Crostoni with Fava Beans and Ricotta Salata	X		
Tomato–Pine Nut Bruschetta	X		
Herbed Goat Cheese with Nasturtiums	X		
Cherry Tomatoes Stuffed with Avocado and Bacon			X
Crostini with Roasted Eggplant, Red Pepper, and Mozzarella	X		
SOMETHING SWEET			
Chocolate-Hazelnut Truffles	X		
Sugar and Spice Walnuts	X		
Lemon-Ginger Madeleines	X		
Mocha Shortbread Buttons	X		

LARGE PLATTERS
AND SMALL BITES

THE MINUTE GUESTS WALK IN THE DOOR, I WANT THEM TO SEE FOOD.

I scatter bowls of olives and nuts about on bookcases and tables in my living room, at eye level and arm's reach, and I put a few more in the kitchen for friends who drift in and out of there. This way, their first small bites will be crunchy and salty, which eases appetites into gear and inevitably leads to drinks. As conversation revs up, people like to cluster and do something with their hands, so I put platters of meats, cheeses, dips, and spreads on a central table, such as in the dining room, or on the cocktail table or kitchen counter, where guests can grab them without thinking and talk at the same time. With music loud enough to set a mood, but low enough to underscore voices, the party is rolling in no time.

Curry Cashews

Watch out . . . these are habit-forming. And great looking, in a Technicolor sort of way.

½ teaspoon ground cumin

½ teaspoon ground coriander

½ teaspoon ground turmeric

½ teaspoon kosher salt

¼ teaspoon cayenne pepper

1 tablespoon butter

1½ cups (6 ounces) whole unsalted cashews

Preheat the oven to 350°F.

    Combine the cumin, coriander, turmeric, salt, and cayenne in a small bowl or ramekin. Place the butter in an 8- or 9-inch pie plate or cake pan and put in the oven. After a few minutes, check to see if the butter has melted. When the butter has melted, remove the pan and add the cashews and spice mix. Toss until the nuts are completely coated with butter and spices. Shake the pan to spread out the nuts, then bake until the nuts are toasted and fragrant, about 12 minutes, shaking the pan once or twice so the nuts cook evenly. Transfer the nuts to a plate and let them cool before serving. (Nuts can be made ahead, cooled, and stored in an airtight container for up to 1 day.)

MAKES 1½ CUPS (12 SERVINGS)
MAKE AHEAD: YES

Spiked Olives

Jazzing up olives makes you feel a bit like a mad scientist in the kitchen. All sorts of herbs and spices work, but this is my favorite combo, with its bright balance of heat, garlic, and citrus. Mix and match green and black olives—kalamata, picholine, luques, gaeta, oil-cured, et cetera—or use premixed olives if your store has an olive bar.

1 ½ cups mixed good-quality olives, drained if necessary

3 tablespoons extra-virgin olive oil

1 clove garlic, minced or pressed

½ teaspoon red pepper flakes

1 lemon

Freshly ground pepper

Mix the olives, oil, garlic, and red pepper flakes in a container with a lid. Remove the zest from the lemon with a zesting tool so it is in very fine strips (if you don't have a zesting tool, grate the lemon zest). Mix in the zest and several grindings of pepper and let the olives stand, covered, at room temperature for at least 2 hours to settle flavors. (Or cover and refrigerate for up to 3 days; let them come to room temperature before serving.)

MAKES ABOUT 1 ½ CUPS (ABOUT 12 SERVINGS)
MAKE AHEAD: YES

Rosemary Almonds

I love sneaking Worcestershire sauce into my recipes. It's one of those ingredients that makes people ask, "What's in this that tastes *so* good?" They'll say it about these nuts, if they can stop eating them long enough to talk.

1 tablespoon butter

1 clove garlic, minced or pressed

1 tablespoon minced fresh rosemary leaves

1 ½ cups (6 ounces) whole unsalted almonds

Salt

2 teaspoons Worcestershire sauce

Preheat the oven to 350°F.

Melt the butter in a large nonstick skillet over medium-high heat. Add the garlic and rosemary and stir a few seconds until fragrant. Add the almonds and salt to taste (be generous) and stir about 1 minute or until the almonds are well coated with butter and spices. Pour in the Worcestershire sauce, shake the pan vigorously, then stir the almonds until glossy, about 1 minute. Pour the nuts onto a baking sheet with sides and place it in the oven; bake until the nuts are toasted and fragrant, about 8 minutes. Let them cool before serving. (Nuts can be stored in an airtight container for up to 2 days.)

MAKES 1 ½ CUPS (12 SERVINGS)
MAKE AHEAD: YES

Dilled Green Beans

I always like something pickled on my appetizer table because that vinegary snap inspires more eating and drinking. Rather than popping open a jar of cornichons, make these incredibly easy beans. The straighter the bean, the better for packing in the jar.

8 ounces very fresh green beans	**1 teaspoon salt**
⅔ cup apple cider vinegar	**3 cloves garlic**
⅔ cup water	**5 sprigs fresh dill**
1 teaspoon sugar	**½ teaspoon red pepper flakes**

Wash a 1-pint canning jar and lid with hot, soapy water, rinse and dry them completely.

Place the beans on a cutting surface with the bottom (curved) ends neatly lined up. Lay the jar down next to the beans, then trim the stemmed tops so the length of the beans is just shorter than the jar. Lay the trimmed beans neatly on a steamer rack in a pan of simmering water and steam, covered, until the beans are crisp-tender, 3 to 5 minutes. Lift out the rack (discard the steaming water) and let the beans stand on the rack. In the same pan, bring the vinegar, water, sugar, and salt to a rolling boil, then remove the pan from the heat.

Pack the beans in the jar, fitting them tightly (if you have extras, eat them). Mash the garlic with the flat side of a chef's knife and discard the skin, then tuck the mashed cloves down among the beans. Tuck in the dill sprigs, then sprinkle in the red pepper. Pour the vinegar mixture into the jar until it reaches the top (you may have extra). Screw on the lid and shake the jar well. Let it stand at room temperature for 8 hours, then transfer the jar to the refrigerator. The beans are ready to eat after 24 hours total and keep, sealed in their jar in the refrigerator, for up to 1 week.

To serve, remove the beans from the liquid and place them in a bowl or glass.

MAKES 1 PINT (8 SERVINGS)
MAKE AHEAD: YES

Warm Green Olives

Heating olives intensifies their flavor and texture. You can use any good unpitted olive, but meaty green olives hold up especially well. Sauté these at the last minute for maximum impact.

2 teaspoons cumin seeds

1½ cups good-quality green olives, such as picholine or luques, drained if necessary

2 tablespoons extra-virgin olive oil

½ teaspoon dried thyme leaves

Freshly ground pepper

1 large navel orange

Put the cumin seeds in a large dry skillet and place over high heat. Toast, shaking the pan a few times, until fragrant, about 1½ minutes. Remove the pan from the heat and add the olives, oil, thyme, and several grindings of pepper. Place over medium heat for 2 or 3 minutes until the olives are hot through, stirring constantly. Transfer them to a bowl, scraping the pan to get all the cumin seeds and oil, then grate orange zest right over the olives; stir well and serve.

MAKES ABOUT 1½ CUPS (ABOUT 12 SERVINGS)
MAKE AHEAD: NO

Gorgonzola Bites

Crunchy and salty, these are always a crowd pleaser, yet it's almost embarrassing to admit how easy they are to make. They're just as good with a fancy blue cheese, such as Gorgonzola, as they are with packaged crumbled blue.

1 sheet (8 ounces) frozen puff pastry

4 ounces Gorgonzola or other blue cheese, crumbled fine

Freshly ground pepper

Preheat the oven to 350°F.

Remove the puff pastry from the package and let it stand at room temperature until pliable (about 30 minutes); unfold it if necessary. Set the pastry sheet on a work surface and scatter the cheese over the pastry, distributing as evenly as possible. Grind a generous amount of pepper over the entire surface. Drape a piece of plastic wrap over the pastry and gently roll over the wrap with a rolling pin to press the cheese into the pastry (the cheese will not cover the entire surface).

Peel off the plastic wrap and cut the pastry into 1-inch squares or diamonds with a sharp knife; discard odd edges and ends. Transfer the pastry pieces, placing them about ½ inch apart, to ungreased baking sheets. Bake until the pastries are puffed and golden, about 25 minutes. Let them cool before serving. (If made ahead, store them in an airtight container for up to 1 day.)

MAKES ABOUT 40 PORTIONS (ABOUT 20 SERVINGS)
MAKE AHEAD: YES

Two-Olive Tapenade

I'm not an anchovy lover, so I make my tapenade with roasted red peppers instead. With olives and capers, it makes for a holy trinity of Mediterranean flavors. Spread on crostini (toasted bread) and garnish with basil to drive the point home. The type of olive used will determine the intensity of this tapenade. Buy whatever kinds you can find pitted, and in a pinch, canned olives are absolutely acceptable.

1 clove garlic

2 tablespoons brined capers, drained

1 ½ cups pitted black olives

1 ½ cups pitted green olives

⅓ cup chopped roasted red bell peppers (jarred okay)

¼ cup chopped fresh basil leaves

⅓ cup extra-virgin olive oil

Toasted baguette slices or crackers

Roughly chop the garlic in a food processor fitted with the metal blade. Add the capers and process until they are finely chopped. Add the olives, bell peppers, and basil and pulse a few times to coarsely chop them. Pour in the oil, then pulse until the mixture is just blended, but not perfectly smooth. Transfer the mixture to a bowl and serve it with baguette slices or crackers. (If made ahead, cover and refrigerate the tapenade for up to 3 days.)

MAKES ABOUT 3 CUPS (ABOUT 12 SERVINGS)
MAKE AHEAD: YES

Roasted Eggplant Dip
with Spiced Pita Crisps

This milder cousin of baba ghanoush has no tahini, so you can fully taste the roasted eggplant. Be generous with the parsley; its fresh green taste pumps up the dip. The crisps are also great with Roasted Tomato Salsa (page 27) or Texas Caviar (page 29) and they can be easily doubled or tripled.

DIP
1 (about 1 pound) Italian eggplant

2 cloves garlic, unpeeled

2 or 3 tablespoons extra-virgin
 olive oil

¼ cup packed fresh Italian
 parsley leaves

1 or 2 tablespoons freshly
 squeezed lemon juice

Salt

PITA CRISPS
Three 6-inch pita breads

Olive or vegetable oil

1 teaspoon kosher salt

½ teaspoon paprika

⅛ teaspoon cayenne pepper

Preheat the oven to 350 °F.

To make the dip: Place the whole eggplant in a baking dish just large enough to hold it and pierce the eggplant 2 or 3 times with the tip of a knife. Place the garlic cloves on a small square of foil and splash them with a bit of oil; enclose the garlic in foil. Put the foil packet in the dish alongside the eggplant and place them in the oven. Bake until the garlic is soft when squeezed (open the packet to test), about 35 minutes. Remove the garlic and let it cool in the foil. Continue to bake the eggplant until it is wrinkled, soft, and almost collapsed, about 25 minutes more. Let it cool in the pan and leave the oven on.

While the eggplant cools, make the pita crisps. Cut the pitas in half and peel them apart to make quarters. Arrange the quarters on a work surface and brush them well with oil. Stir together the salt, paprika, and cayenne in a small ramekin or bowl and sprinkle them over the pita quarters. Stack and cut the pita into wedges (you should get 3 wedges per quarter, or 36 total).

(continued)

Spread the wedges on baking sheets and bake them until crisp and golden, about 12 minutes. (Crisps can be cooled and stored airtight for up to 2 days.)

Cut the stem off the cooled eggplant and pull off and discard the skin. Chop the flesh and set it aside. Peel the garlic cloves and put them in a food processor fitted with the metal blade. Add the parsley and pulse until it is finely chopped. Add the chopped eggplant, 1 tablespoon of the lemon juice, and 2 tablespoons of the extra-virgin olive oil; pulse until just combined (do not purée). Taste the dip and add salt and more lemon juice and/or oil as needed. Pulse again until the mixture is almost smooth; it should have the texture of guacamole. (If made ahead, transfer the dip to a bowl and wrap it with plastic, pressing the wrap right onto the surface. Refrigerate for up to 2 days.)

Serve the dip in a bowl surrounded with the pita crisps.

MAKES 12 SERVINGS
MAKE AHEAD: YES

Roasted Tomato Salsa

Purchased salsa is so easy to find now that it's not worth making your own unless it is exceptional—and this one is. Dry roasting mellows the flavors and adds a smoky dimension that is then amplified by chipotles, or canned smoked jalapeño peppers. If you don't have an iron skillet, hold the vegetables with tongs and char them over a gas burner.

1 ½ pounds firm-ripe tomatoes

1 small red onion, unpeeled, quartered

2 cloves garlic, unpeeled

½ cup packed fresh cilantro leaves

1 canned chipotle in adobo sauce

1 tablespoon vegetable oil

1 lime

Salt

Tortilla chips

Place a large dry cast-iron skillet over medium-high heat. Place the tomatoes, onion, and garlic in the pan and roast, turning as needed with tongs, until blistered and charred all over. Let the vegetables cool slightly, then pull off their skins and discard. Cut the tomatoes in half crosswise and gently squeeze them over a sink to extract their seeds.

In a blender or food processor fitted with the metal blade, combine the roasted vegetables with the cilantro and chipotle. Pulse until they are coarsely chopped. Transfer the mixture to a bowl and stir in the oil; squeeze lime juice into the salsa to taste. Season to taste with salt. (If made ahead, cover, and refrigerate for up to 3 days.)

Serve the salsa in a bowl surrounded by chips.

MAKES ABOUT 3 CUPS (ABOUT 12 SERVINGS)
MAKE AHEAD: YES

Texas Caviar

In Texas, this is served on New Year's Day to bring good luck. I like it anytime for casual parties as a break from salsa. Plus, my guests crack up when they figure out that what Texans call "caviar" is, in fact, black-eyed peas.

One 15-ounce can black-eyed peas

8 ounces ripe red tomatoes

1 celery stalk, finely diced

¼ cup minced red onion

1 small jalapeño pepper, seeded and minced

2 tablespoons minced fresh cilantro leaves (optional)

1½ tablespoons apple cider vinegar

2 teaspoons olive oil

¼ teaspoon ground cumin

Salt

Tabasco sauce

Tortilla chips or Pita Crisps (page 24)

Put the black-eyed peas in a sieve and rinse them well under cold water; shake to get rid of excess water. Place them in a mixing bowl. Core the tomatoes, then cut them in half crosswise and squeeze them gently over a sink to extract their seeds. Finely chop the tomatoes and add to the bowl with the peas. Stir in the celery, red onion, jalapeño, cilantro (if using), vinegar, oil, and cumin. Season the mixture to taste with salt and Tabasco sauce. (If made ahead, cover and refrigerate for up to 1 day.)

Serve the "caviar" in a bowl surrounded with tortilla chips or pita crisps.

MAKES ABOUT 3 CUPS (ABOUT 12 SERVINGS)
MAKE AHEAD: YES

Salumi with Italian Salsa

One of the most natural entertainers I know, Lori Hunter, sets out prosciutto, chunks of Parmigiano-Reggiano, bread, and what she calls "Italian Salsa" at her big kitchen island. Everybody picks and chooses what combination appeals to them and everybody is happy. I add a few more cold cuts to make this a true selection of "salumi" (the Italian word for cured meats), and I toast the bread as for crostini (you can leave it untoasted if you prefer).

ITALIAN SALSA
1 pound ripe tomatoes

½ cup lightly packed fresh basil leaves

1 tablespoon extra-virgin olive oil

1 clove garlic, minced or pressed

Salt

1 loaf crusty Italian bread

Extra-virgin olive oil

2 bulbs fennel (optional)

8 ounces Parmigiano-Reggiano cheese

1 pound thinly sliced Italian cured meats, such as salami, prosciutto, and s*oppressata*

To make the salsa: Core, seed, and chop the tomatoes by hand (do not use a food processor as they will get too watery). Stack the basil leaves and cut them in half lengthwise, then slice them crosswise into very fine shreds. Put the tomatoes, basil, oil, and garlic in a decorative bowl. Mix gently, then season to taste with salt. Set aside.

Preheat a broiler and adjust the rack so it is about 4 inches from the heating element. Cut the bread into ½-inch-thick slices, brush them on both sides with oil, and broil, turning once, until they are golden. (Recipe can be made ahead up to this point. Let the bread and the tomato mixture stand separately at room temperature for up 3 hours.)

Cut the stems and fronds off the fennel (if using), trim off the bases, and cut the bulbs in half lengthwise. Slice them thinly crosswise. Break the cheese into small chunks with the tip of a knife. Arrange the sliced fennel, meats, and cheese on a board or large platter with the bowl of Italian Salsa. Offer the toasted bread alongside.

MAKES 12 SERVINGS
MAKE AHEAD: YES

Oysters with Preserved–Meyer Lemon Mignonette

Classic *mignonette* sauce for oysters is made with shallots, wine vinegar, and pepper. You can use that basic formula if you don't want to go to the trouble of preserving lemons (which must be done well in advance), but you will miss out. The tart-salty bits of lemon are like sparks with the sweet oysters. Have the fishmonger shuck the oysters; it can be frustrating to do yourself.

PRESERVED LEMONS
8 to 10 organically grown Meyer lemons

Kosher salt

Boiling water

MIGNONETTE
1 Preserved Lemon (left)

3 tablespoons champagne vinegar

1 teaspoon minced shallot

Freshly ground pepper

2 dozen shucked oysters in their shells

Cracked ice

To make the preserved lemons: Wash a 1-pint glass jar and lid with hot, soapy water; rinse and dry them thoroughly. Set out a large piece of parchment or waxed paper to work over.

Cut a lemon into fourths through 1 end, but do not cut all the way through the other end. You want it to open out like a flower, but not to come apart. Place the lemon on the paper, spread it open, and sprinkle it with a heaping tablespoon of kosher salt; place the lemon in the jar. Repeat 1 by 1 with the remaining lemons, sprinkling salt on each one. Pack the lemons into the jar tightly, filling it to the top (you may use up to 6 lemons, depending on size). When you reach the top, lift the paper and pour any excess salt from it into the jar. Pour boiling water into the jar until it reaches about halfway up. Then juice the remaining lemons 1 by 1, adding the juice to the jar until it reaches the top. Seal the jar, shake it well, and let it stand at room temperature, shaking well every 24 hours, for 1 week. Transfer the jar to the refrigerator, continuing to shake it every other day. The lemons are ready after 3 weeks and keep several months in the refrigerator.

To make the mignonette: Pull out ¼ of 1 of the preserved lemons. Scrape and discard the pulp from the peel. With a sharp paring knife, slice the peel into tiny strips lengthwise, then cut them crosswise to create tiny dice; you should have about 2 teaspoons. In a measuring cup, mix the vinegar, preserved lemon peel, shallot, and several grindings of pepper. Pour into a small shallow dish or ramekin. Set the oysters on a cupped platter or tray lined with cracked ice; snuggle the mignonette in the center.

Serve with tiny forks to eat the oysters. Or, loosen each oyster completely from its shell, top each with a spoonful of mignonette, and serve without forks.

MAKES 24 PORTIONS (12 SERVINGS)
MAKE AHEAD: LEMONS ONLY

Roasted Vegetable Platter with Arugula Green Goddess Dip

You can find root vegetables in grocery stores the year round, but here's a good reason to visit the farmers' market in colder months (when farmers need your business most). There you will find glorious multicolored beets, sweet young carrots, and electric-green arugula for a platter that is a play on crudités. The dip is even better made the day ahead.

ARUGULA GREEN GODDESS DIP

¾ cup sour cream

¼ cup mayonnaise

1 green onion, including top, chopped

1 clove garlic, chopped

1 tablespoon freshly squeezed lemon juice

2 cups (about 2 ounces) packed fresh arugula leaves

2 tablespoons chopped fresh tarragon leaves

Salt

VEGETABLES

6 large or 12 small beets, in mixed colors if possible

4 (about 1½ pounds) parsnips

24 (about 1 pound) baby carrots (not bagged mini-carrots) or 12 regular carrots

2 celery roots

Olive oil

Salt

24 very small (about 1½ pounds) red or white "creamer" or Yukon gold potatoes

To make the dip: Combine the sour cream, mayonnaise, onion, garlic, and lemon juice in a blender or food processor fitted with the metal blade. Add half of the arugula and pulse until just combined; add the remaining arugula and the tarragon and pulse until just combined. Season to taste with salt. Transfer the dip to a bowl or decorative container, cover, and refrigerate while you prepare the vegetables, or for up to 1 day.

To prepare the vegetables: Preheat the oven (with 2 racks) to 375°F. Trim the leaves and stems off the vegetables and wash the vegetables

(continued)

well. Wrap half of the beets in a large piece of aluminum foil and set them in the oven directly on 1 rack; repeat with the other beets, putting them on the other rack.

Peel the parsnips and carrots. If using baby carrots, leave them whole. If using larger carrots, cut them into sticks about 3 inches long and ½ inch thick. With a chef's knife, cut the bottom and top off of the celery roots, then trim away the peel. Cut the parsnips and celery roots in pieces about the same size as the carrots (the vegetables need to be roughly the same size so that they cook evenly). Keep each of the vegetables separate. Toss the carrots in a small bowl with 2 teaspoons oil and a generous pinch of salt, then place them on a baking sheet in 1 layer. Repeat with the celery roots and transfer them to the same baking sheet, but keep the vegetables separate. Repeat with the parsnips, then transfer them to another baking sheet. Repeat with the potatoes (leave them whole), then place them on the baking sheet with the parsnips, keeping the vegetables separate. Place the baking sheets in the oven alongside the beets.

After 30 minutes, test the carrots, celery roots, and parsnips for doneness; they should be cooked through and slightly browned, but not soft. Remove any cooked vegetables and return the pans to the oven as necessary for another 5 minutes or so until the remaining vegetables are done. Test the potatoes and beets after 45 minutes; if a knife slides easily into the centers, they are done (beets may need up to an hour, depending on size). Let the vegetables stand at room temperature. When the beets are cool enough to handle, pull off the skins and cut the beets into wedges. (The vegetables can be cooked up to 2 hours ahead and left standing at room temperature.)

Arrange the vegetables in groups on a platter and serve with the dip.

MAKES 12 SERVINGS
MAKE AHEAD: YES

Goat Cheese with Cumin and Mint

Years ago when I worked for *Sunset,* this recipe came out in the magazine. It's been a regular at my parties since and it's the only "cheese and cracker" combination I serve.

1 large log (about 11 ounces) fresh goat cheese

2 tablespoons cumin seeds

Freshly ground pepper

3 tablespoons extra-virgin olive oil

¼ cup minced fresh mint leaves, plus mint sprigs for garnish

Seeded crackers, such as Ak-Mak

Place the goat cheese log on a plate. Sprinkle it with the cumin seeds and generous grindings of pepper, then roll the log to press the seeds into the cheese. (If made ahead, cover with plastic wrap and refrigerate for up to 2 hours.) Transfer the cheese to a serving plate, drizzle it with the oil, and sprinkle it with the minced mint. Surround the cheese with crackers and garnish the plate with mint sprigs.

MAKES 8 SERVINGS
MAKE AHEAD: YES

Seasonal Cheese and Fruit

Is it a cliché . . . or still the most popular food at a party? That depends on what you select for a cheese platter. Today, with the incredible renaissance of artisanal cheesemaking, your choices are superb.

For a cheese platter, limit yourself to no more than four selections, or your guests will be overwhelmed. I like a mix of sheep, goat, and cow's milk cheeses, including one firm, aged cheese; one blue variety; one soft-ripened or creamy cheese; and one cheese I've never had before, just for fun. Try a combination of shapes (wedges, pyramids, logs, and small wheels) and tones for visual variety. Always let cheese come to room temperature before serving or the flavors won't shine. Don't worry about leftovers; you can always find a use for them.

Another option is to focus on one cheese paired with a fruit, nut, or meat that particularly complements it. Here are some favorites that work in different seasons. I don't serve bread with all of these—I like to encourage guests to use their hands and taste the cheese, then the other ingredients—but if you want to offer bread alongside, go ahead (crackers tend to be a bit too cardboardy). For amazing chile jams, go to www.tierravegetables.com.

ITALIAN PLATE

8 ounces Parmigiano-Reggiano
  or grana padano cheese

12 thin slices prosciutto

6 ripe figs, quartered

1 cup fresh blackberries, if available

SPANISH PLATE

8 ounces manchego cheese

About 4 ounces quince paste
  (*membrillo*, available at many
  cheese shops and gourmet stores)

About 6 ounces Cabrales (Spanish
  blue) or other blue cheese

1 tablespoon chestnut honey or
  other dark honey

1 cup (4 ounces) whole walnuts

CALIFORNIA PLATE

8 ounces Teleme or Taleggio cheese

12 dried apricots

¼ cup top-quality chile jam (see
  headnote)

12 or more thin slices walnut
  bread, toasted

DESSERT PLATE

8 ounces mascarpone cheese

8 ounces ripe Bing or other sweet
  cherries

1 cup (4 ounces) whole pecans

For the Italian Plate: Arrange the cheese, prosciutto, and figs on a platter. Scatter the blackberries all around, if using. To eat, nibble the cheese, meat, and fruit together in any combination.

For the Spanish Plate: Cut the manchego cheese into ¼-inch-thick slices or triangles, then slice the quince paste about ⅛ inch thick and cut into strips ¼ inch wide to make little rectangles to go on top of each piece of manchego cheese (trim length if necessary). Place the quince paste strips on top of the cheese and put them on a plate. Put the blue cheese on the same plate and drizzle it lightly with the honey; mound the walnuts alongside. Eat the manchego with the quince. Eat the blue cheese and honey with the walnuts.

For the California Plate: Arrange the cheese and apricots on a plate. Put the jam in a ramekin on the plate and arrange the bread around the sides. To eat, spread some jam on bread, top with cheese, and eat with an apricot.

For the Dessert Plate: Spoon the cheese into a small bowl or ramekin, fluffing it attractively. Mound the cherries and pecans alongside. To eat, spread some mascarpone on a pecan and eat with a cherry (offer a small bowl alongside for cherry stems and pits).

MAKES 6 SERVINGS EACH
MAKE AHEAD: NO

WARM
FINGER FOODS

AS THESE COME OUT OF THE KITCHEN HOT AND SMELLING

divine, a mob scene forms around each plateful. Pass them by hand so everyone gets some, returning to the kitchen as needed to refill. If you don't want to be the server, ask your son, daughter, niece, or nephew to help out, or pay a neighborhood kid to come over, or even ask a guest to pass, especially some-one shy (who needs to be nudged to mingle) or someone outrageously gregarious (who wants to say hello to every person in the room). When planning a party menu, the impulse is strong to choose a lot of warm appetizers since they are so irresistible, but it's a good idea to limit yourself to two or three. Otherwise, you could end up in the kitchen all night and miss the fun of the party.

Baby Lamb Chops with Mint-Cilantro Relish

Splurge on tiny, two-bite lamb chops for the most elegant occasions. Ask the butcher to remove as much of the fat from the ribs and meat as possible—a term referred to as "Frenching." I like to pass these on small plates, such as saucers, so each guest has a place to put the bone when she's finished.

MINT-CILANTRO RELISH
¼ cup freshly squeezed lime juice

2 green onions, including tops, sliced

1 serrano chile, stemmed and seeded

1 clove garlic

1-inch piece fresh ginger, peeled and halved

Salt

1 teaspoon sugar

1 cup tightly packed fresh mint leaves

1 cup tightly packed fresh cilantro leaves

2 racks lamb, well trimmed of fat

Olive oil

Freshly ground pepper

To make the relish: In a blender, blend the lime juice, onions, chile, garlic, ginger, 1 teaspoon salt, sugar, and 2 tablespoons water. Scrape down the container, add the mint and cilantro, and purée. Refrigerate, covered, until the mixture thickens and the flavors settle, about 1 hour (but not more or the sauce will darken).

To prepare the lamb chops: Preheat the oven to 500°F. Place the lamb racks on a plate and rub them all over with oil, then salt and pepper them generously. When the oven is hot, place a baking sheet in it for 5 minutes, then place the racks, fat sides down, directly on the hot pan. Roast until a meat thermometer inserted in the thickest part of the meat registers 135°F, about 12 minutes. Remove the pan and let the lamb stand in the pan until ready to serve, up to 15 minutes.

Slice the chops between the bones, place each chop on a small plate, and spoon the sauce alongside. Serve immediately.

MAKES 16 PORTIONS (8 SERVINGS)
MAKE AHEAD: RELISH ONLY

Cornmeal Blini with Smoked Salmon

Put an American spin on blini with fresh corn and *masa harina* (corn flour for tortillas, available at most supermarkets). I adore them with smoked salmon, but if you are a caviar lover, use it.

BLINI

½ cup all-purpose flour

½ cup masa harina

1 teaspoon sugar

1 teaspoon baking powder

½ teaspoon salt

½ cup white corn kernels (from about ½ ear)

1 cup buttermilk

1 large egg

2 tablespoons melted butter, plus additional melted butter for cooking blini

GARNISHES

½ cup crème fraîche

Smoked salmon (about ½ pound) or caviar to taste (1 or 2 ounces)

1 bunch fresh chives, finely snipped

To make the blini: Stir the flour, masa harina, sugar, baking powder, and salt together in a large bowl. Put the corn kernels in a blender and purée them until pulpy. Add the buttermilk, egg, and 2 tablespoons melted butter and pulse just to blend. Pour the buttermilk mixture into the dry ingredients and stir to combine.

Place a nonstick skillet over medium-high heat. Brush the pan lightly with melted butter, then make small pancakes with the batter, using about 1 tablespoon batter per cake. Cook until the tops of the cakes start to look dry and the bottoms are golden brown, then flip them over and cook until they are golden brown on the other side, about 3 minutes total. Transfer the cooked blini to an ovenproof plate and store it in a low (250 °F) oven while you cook the remaining cakes. (Blini can be made ahead, cooled, stored airtight in plastic bags, and refrigerated for up to 1 day, or frozen for up to 1 month. Reheat in a low oven [thawed if frozen] until just warm.)

To serve, top each blini with some crème fraîche and salmon or caviar and sprinkle with the chives.

MAKES ABOUT 20 BLINI (ABOUT 10 SERVINGS)
MAKE AHEAD: YES

Tandoori Chicken Spears

You can serve this Indian-inspired recipe several ways. Speared with a tooth-pick, it is very manageable and a good choice if you have a lot of bread-based appetizers already on the menu. You can also pass the chicken on pita crisps for a more casual look, or cut it into strips instead of chunks and thread it onto skewers for a satay-style presentation.

TANDOORI MARINADE
¼ cup plain lowfat yogurt

1-inch piece fresh ginger, peeled

1 clove garlic

1 teaspoon paprika

½ teaspoon ground cumin

½ teaspoon ground turmeric

¼ teaspoon cayenne pepper

**2 skinless, boneless chicken
  breast halves**

Salt

1 bottle top-quality mango chutney

1 bunch fresh cilantro

Pita Crisps (page 24) (optional)

To make the marinade: In a blender, purée the yogurt, ginger, garlic, paprika, cumin, turmeric, and cayenne. Set the marinade aside.

Pull the filet off the back side of each chicken breast. Cut the breasts and filets into 1-inch chunks. (For skewers, pound the chicken breasts between pieces of waxed paper or plastic wrap until about ½ inch thick, then cut them into strips about 1 inch wide.) Place the chicken chunks or strips in the mari-nade, season well with salt, stir, and refrigerate, covered, for at least 30 minutes or up to 3 hours.

To serve, preheat a broiler and adjust the rack so it is about 4 inches from the heating element (if using wooden skewers, soak the skewers in warm water for at least 30 minutes before using).

For chicken spears, lift the chunks from the marinade with a slotted spoon and place them on a nonstick or oiled baking sheet, setting them about ½ inch apart, working in batches. Broil until they are cooked through, about 8 minutes, turning the pieces halfway through. Use the tip of a grapefruit knife to scoop out a chunk of mango from the chutney bottle and place it on top of each chicken chunk. Pluck off a cilantro leaf and place it on top of the chutney and spear the leaf, chutney, and chicken together with a toothpick. (Offer guests a small container or glass for depositing used toothpicks.)

To serve on pita crisps, prepare those ahead of time. Broil the chicken chunks as directed above. Place a cilantro leaf on each crisp, top with a piece of chicken and a dab of chutney.

For skewers, thread marinated chicken strips onto soaked skewers, weaving the skewer in and out so the meat lies flat. Broil, turning once, until cooked through, about 8 minutes. Place them on a platter lined with cilantro sprigs and place a small bowl of chutney in the center for dipping.

MAKES ABOUT 24 PORTIONS (ABOUT 12 SERVINGS)
MAKE AHEAD: MARINATING ONLY

Merguez Meatballs with Yogurt Sauce

Meatballs are a cocktail party standard, but this version, dunked into minty yogurt sauce, is hardly predictable. The spicing takes its cue from *merguez,* a type of Moroccan sausage. The meat will taste best if blended up to a day in advance, but cooked at the last possible moment or it will dry out.

MEATBALLS

1 pound ground lamb or beef (not too lean)

2 cloves garlic, minced or pressed

2 tablespoons chopped fresh cilantro leaves

2 tablespoons red wine vinegar

1 tablespoon paprika

2 teaspoons ground cumin

2 teaspoons ground coriander

1 ½ teaspoons salt

Freshly ground pepper

YOGURT SAUCE

1 cup plain lowfat yogurt

½ cup loosely packed fresh mint leaves

½ cup loosely packed fresh cilantro leaves

To make the meatballs: Put the meat in a large bowl and add the garlic, cilantro, vinegar, paprika, cumin, coriander, salt, and a generous grinding of pepper. Mix it with your hands until well blended. Set aside.

To make the sauce: Blend the yogurt, mint, and cilantro in a food processor fitted with the metal blade, or in a blender. (Meat mixture and sauce can each be made up to 1 day ahead, covered, and refrigerated separately.)

To serve, preheat a broiler and adjust the rack so it is about 4 inches from the heating element. Form the meat mixture into 1-inch meatballs and place them on a baking sheet with sides (work in batches if necessary). Broil the meatballs until they are no longer pink inside, about 8 minutes, shaking the pan once or twice so the meatballs cook evenly. Transfer them to paper towels to drain.

Skewer the meatballs with toothpicks and serve them immediately on a platter with the yogurt sauce in a small bowl alongside. (Offer guests a small container or glass for depositing used toothpicks.)

MAKES ABOUT 40 PORTIONS (ABOUT 20 SERVINGS)
MAKE AHEAD: MEAT MIXTURE AND SAUCE

Chorizo and Potatoes with Romesco

For this tapas-style appetizer, pass roasted tiny potatoes and chunks of grilled sausage with bowls of Spanish red pepper dip called *romesco* (if your guests are dressed up, offer them toothpicks for the dunking).

ROMESCO

1 small red bell pepper

⅓ cup (1½ ounces) whole almonds

1 clove garlic

1 cup mayonnaise

1 tablespoon sherry vinegar or red wine vinegar

Salt

24 very small (about 1½ pounds) red or white "creamer," Yukon gold, and/or purple potatoes

Extra-virgin olive oil

1 pound chorizo sausages (or other spicy pork sausages)

To make the romesco: Preheat a broiler and adjust the rack so it is about 4 inches from the heating element. Cut the red pepper into quarters around the core; discard the stem and seeds. Put the pepper pieces, skin sides up, on a baking sheet and broil until the skins are charred, about 7 minutes. Transfer the peppers to a plastic bag and close the bag. Let the peppers steam until cool to the touch, then pull off the charred skin and chop the peppers.

Place the almonds and the garlic in a food processor fitted with the metal blade; process until the nuts are finely ground (do not let them turn to paste). Add the peppers, mayonnaise, vinegar, and a hefty pinch of salt; process until blended but not perfectly smooth. Transfer the sauce to a bowl and cover with plastic wrap. Refrigerate at least 2 hours or for up to 3 days.

About an hour before serving, preheat the oven to 375°F. Spread the potatoes on a baking sheet. Drizzle them with oil and sprinkle with salt, then shake the pan to coat the potatoes. Roast until the potatoes are soft inside and crispy outside (30 to 40 minutes). During the last 10 minutes, cook the chorizo in a broiler or on a grill until cooked through and crackly, 7 to 10 minutes. Cut the chorizo into ½-inch-thick slices. Cut the potatoes in half. Arrange the sausages and potatoes on a platter or plates and serve with the romesco.

MAKES 24 PORTIONS (12 SERVINGS)
MAKE AHEAD: ROMESCO ONLY

Salt-Roasted Prawns with Lemon Pesto

Chef Bibby Gignilliat offers these at her "Gourmet Gatherings" cooking parties in San Francisco. The salt-roasting keeps the prawns moist and tender, and the pesto is the best I've tasted. Serve the prawns in the baking dish and provide discard bowls for the shells. If it's a dressier affair, peel off the shells down to the last segment right above the tails.

LEMON PESTO

1 lemon

1 ½ cups tightly packed fresh basil leaves

⅓ cup (about 1 ½ ounces) freshly grated Parmesan cheese

⅓ cup extra-virgin olive oil

¼ cup (1 ounce) toasted pine nuts

1 clove garlic

½ teaspoon salt

Pinch of freshly ground pepper

About 3 cups rock salt

24 medium prawns or shrimp in shells

To make the pesto: Grate the zest from the lemon and squeeze 2 tablespoons of the juice. Put the basil, cheese, oil, pine nuts, lemon zest, lemon juice, garlic, salt, and pepper in a food processor fitted with the metal blade and process until the mixture forms a smooth paste. (Pesto can be made ahead, transferred to a bowl, covered, and refrigerated for up to 1 day.)

Preheat the oven to 550 °F. Spread the rock salt in the bottom of a 10-inch gratin dish or other shallow decorative ovenproof dish; the salt should be about ¾ inch thick. Place prawns in a single layer, on their sides, directly on the salt, pushing them down slightly to partially bury them. Roast until the prawns are pink, 3 to 5 minutes. Remove the dish and let the prawns cool a few minutes. Place the pesto in a small heatproof bowl and nestle it in the center of the baking dish with the prawns and salt around it; serve immediately. (Or, if desired, remove the prawns, cut down the backs of the shells with sharp kitchen scissors, and peel off the shells to just above the tails. Serve the peeled shrimp on a platter with the pesto.)

MAKES 24 PORTIONS (12 SERVINGS)
MAKE AHEAD: PESTO ONLY

Wild Mushroom Croustades

Toasted bread cups, or *croustades,* are a French hors d'oeuvres I learned in cooking school and a concept I think should be brought back. They're far easier to make than pastry tartlets and they can hold creamy, rich fillings. For these, I use a mix of inexpensive white or brown regular mushrooms with whatever seasonal wild mushrooms I can find, such as chanterelles, oyster mushrooms, or morels. Don't ignore the nutmeg; it lifts all the other flavors (and is best when freshly grated).

24 thin slices white bread

8 ounces (white or brown) mushrooms

4 ounces wild mushrooms

2 tablespoons butter

1 large shallot, minced

¼ cup dry sherry

½ cup heavy (whipping) cream

2 tablespoons chopped fresh Italian parsley leaves

1 teaspoon fresh or ½ teaspoon dried thyme leaves

Salt

Freshly ground pepper

Freshly grated nutmeg (or ground nutmeg)

2 tablespoons freshly grated Parmesan cheese

Preheat the oven to 400 °F. Using a 2½-inch round cutter, cut a circle of bread from each slice (save leftover bread for croutons or bread crumbs). Snuggle the bread rounds into mini-muffin tins, pressing gently to mold to the cups. Bake the bread until golden brown, about 12 minutes. Set aside in the tins.

Meanwhile, wipe the mushroom caps clean with a damp paper towel (check the gills of the wild mushrooms carefully for dirt). Trim off the tough ends of the stems, then finely chop the caps and moist stems by hand or in a food processor fitted with the metal blade.

Melt the butter in a large skillet over medium-high heat, add the shallot, and stir 1 minute until fragrant. Stir in the mushrooms, then cover and cook the mushrooms for about 3 minutes or until they soften. Remove the cover and increase the heat to high, letting any liquid evaporate, then pour in the sherry. Boil for 30 seconds, then stir in the cream, parsley, and thyme. Cook, stirring occasionally, until the mixture thickens, about 3 minutes. Remove from the heat and season it well with salt, pepper, and several gratings of fresh nutmeg (or a pinch of ground). Stir well.

Preheat a broiler and adjust the rack so it is about 4 inches from the heating element. Remove the bread cups from the tins and fill them evenly with the mushroom mixture. Sprinkle each with some Parmesan, then place them on a baking sheet. Broil until they are browned on top, about 2 minutes. Serve warm.

MAKES 24 PORTIONS (12 SERVINGS)
MAKE AHEAD: NO

Tomato-Gruyère Tart Squares

Even though you can make this tart ahead, it would be very strategic to have it baking in the oven when guests arrive because it smells incredible. This is a perfect choice for a summer party during the glut of heirloom tomatoes, but it also works with Roma tomatoes any time of year.

1 sheet (8 ounces) frozen puff pastry

1 tablespoon Dijon mustard

1 large shallot, minced

1 cup (about 4 ounces) shredded Gruyère cheese

1 pound ripe heirloom or Roma tomatoes

½ teaspoon fresh or ¼ teaspoon dried thyme leaves

Salt

Freshly ground pepper

Preheat the oven to 375 °F.

Remove the puff pastry from the package and let it stand at room temperature until pliable (about 30 minutes); unfold if necessary. Set the pastry sheet on a work surface. With a rolling pin, press it into a slightly larger rectangle, about 11 by 10 inches. Lift the pastry gently and transfer it to a baking sheet. Spread the mustard in a thin layer to within ½ inch from the edge of the pastry. Sprinkle the shallots, then the shredded cheese, over the mustard, also covering to ½ inch from the edge of the pastry.

Cut the heirloom tomatoes in half crosswise and gently squeeze them over a sink to extract their seeds. With a sharp knife, thinly slice the tomatoes. (If using Roma tomatoes, core and thinly slice them crosswise.) Arrange the tomatoes on top of the cheese in 3 or more vertical rows, slightly overlapping them as necessary and covering to ½ inch from the edge of the pastry. Sprinkle the thyme, and salt and pepper to taste over the tomatoes. Fold in the edges of the pastry to the tomatoes; it does not have to be perfectly neat. Bake the tart until the edges turn golden brown, 25 to 30 minutes. Remove the tart and let it stand until cooled slightly. Put the tart on a cutting board and cut into 16 squares. Serve warm. (Tart can be made up to 4 hours ahead and reheated in a 300 °F oven until warm.)

MAKES 16 PORTIONS (8 SERVINGS)
MAKE AHEAD: YES

Arancini

It seems like we rarely fry anymore, so I hope these risotto fritters inspire you to make an exception. The name alone will get cocktail conversation bubbling: *arancini* means "little oranges" in Italian—a reference to their golden color— but they're sometimes called *supplí al telefono,* or "telephone wires," a play on the mozzarella strings that hang when you bite one in half. For the crunchiest surface, use Japanese panko bread crumbs (available in many supermarkets).

The risotto for these is made using a shortcut to save time and it must be chilled well in advance of frying the balls. If you have leftover risotto, this is a great way to use it up.

SAFFRON RISOTTO
3 cups chicken or vegetable broth

Pinch of saffron threads

1 tablespoon butter

2 tablespoons olive oil

1 small yellow onion, chopped

¾ cup Arborio rice

⅓ cup (about 1½ ounces) freshly grated Parmesan cheese

ARANCINI
2 ounces part-skim or whole-milk mozzarella cheese

2 large eggs

1½ cups panko or fine dry bread crumbs

⅓ cup all-purpose flour

Vegetable oil

Several hours or up to 1 day before serving, make the risotto: In a medium saucepan, bring the broth to a boil. Stir in the saffron, then turn off the heat. Leave the broth on a back burner. On a front burner, melt the butter in the oil in a medium sauté pan or skillet over medium-high heat. Add the onion and cook, stirring, until soft, about 3 minutes. Add the rice and stir until it is well coated with the oil and butter, about 2 minutes. Ladle in ½ cup of the broth and cook, stirring, until it is absorbed. Repeat this 3 more times, stirring constantly and only adding more broth once the previous amount has been absorbed. Now pour in the remaining broth, bring to a boil, stirring, then reduce the heat, cover, and cook 12 minutes or until the liquid is absorbed and the rice is tender. Transfer the risotto to a mixing bowl and stir in the cheese. Cool to room temperature, then refrigerate, covered, until cold, at least 5 hours or up to 1 day.

To make the arancini: Cut the mozzarella into sixteen ½-inch cubes. Scoop up a heaping tablespoon of the cold risotto and pass it back and forth between your hands to shape it into a ball about 1½ inches in diameter. Push a cube of mozzarella into the center of the rice, then press and seal the rice around the cheese to reform a ball. Continue with the remaining rice and cheese, placing the balls on a plate or tray as they are made.

In a shallow bowl or soup plate, beat the eggs to blend. Place the bread crumbs and flour on separate plates and line up the eggs, flour, and crumbs near the stove.

Pour enough oil into a medium, heavy saucepan to measure ½ inch deep. Over medium-high heat, bring the oil to 325 °F on a deep-frying thermometer. Meanwhile, gently roll a risotto ball in the flour to coat it lightly, transfer it to the beaten eggs and turn with a fork to coat, lift out with the fork, and roll it in the bread crumbs. Place the coated ball back on the plate or tray. Continue with the remaining balls. When the oil is ready, drop in a few balls and cook until they are golden brown all over, turning as needed to brown evenly, about 3 to 4 minutes total. Transfer them to a paper towel–lined ovenproof plate and store in a low (250 °F) oven while you cook the remaining arancini. Serve warm.

MAKES 16 PORTIONS (8 SERVINGS)
MAKE AHEAD: RISOTTO ONLY

Cheddar-Chive Gougères

Making pâte à choux was one of the first things I learned in cooking school and I've had the pastry formula rattling around in my head ever since. When flavored with cheese and baked, it puffs into addictive *gougères*. The French tend to make theirs with Gruyère, I use Cheddar, and either way, they beg to be eaten with Pinot Noir. For parties, I make one-bite gougères and people tend to eat 3 or 4. You can also split these and fill them with chicken, ham, or lobster salad for substantial hors d'oeuvres.

1 cup water

1 stick (8 tablespoons) unsalted
  butter, cut into pieces

½ teaspoon salt

1 cup all-purpose flour

4 large eggs

1 ½ teaspoons dry mustard

¼ teaspoon cayenne pepper

1 ½ cups (about 6 ounces) shredded
  sharp Cheddar cheese

2 tablespoons minced fresh chives

Preheat the oven to 375 °F. Line 2 baking sheets with parchment paper.

Put the water, butter, and salt in a medium, heavy saucepan and place over medium-high heat. Cook, swirling the pan a few times until the butter melts; once it has melted, increase the heat to high and bring the mixture to a rolling boil. Turn off the heat and dump in the flour. Beat the mixture with a wooden spoon until it starts to pull away from the sides of the pan. Take the pan off the stove, set it on a counter or hot pad, and let it cool, without stirring, for 5 minutes.

Now work in the eggs, 1 at a time, beating the mixture well with the spoon after each addition (you have to put some muscle into it to incorporate the eggs fully). With each addition, the dough should look glossy and slick at first, then stick to the sides of the pan before you add the next egg. After beating in the last egg, beat in the dry mustard and cayenne, then the cheese and chives.

Scoop up a heaping teaspoon of dough and with another spoon, push it off onto the paper-lined baking sheet (it should form a mound about 1 inch in diameter). Continue with the remaining dough, leaving an inch of space

(continued)

between the gougères (work in batches as necessary; the dough can stand, covered with buttered waxed paper or parchment, for up to ½ hour). Bake until the gougères are puffy and light golden, about 25 minutes, switching pan positions halfway through. Remove from oven and let cool slightly before serving, or turn off oven and let gougères remain in oven, with door ajar, for up to 1 hour.

MAKES 40 TO 50 GOUGÈRES (ABOUT 15 SERVINGS)
MAKE AHEAD: YES

Warm Dates with Sea Salt and Lime

I have eaten dates all my life, but I never really *tasted* them until renowned food writer Patricia Wells taught me to sauté them. Warmed up, they are the sexiest appetizer imaginable.

12 dates, preferably Medjool

12 to 24 whole roasted, unsalted almonds

2 tablespoons extra-virgin olive oil

Sea salt

Grated zest of 1 lime

Slit the side of each date with a paring knife and spread it open to pull out the pit. Insert an almond in the cavity (2 if the date is large) and push the edges of the date back together to enclose the nut(s).

In a small nonstick skillet, warm the oil over medium heat. Add the dates and cook, shaking the pan so the dates roll around in the oil, until the dates are warmed through, 2 to 3 minutes. Using tongs, transfer the dates to a plate. Sprinkle them lightly with salt and a pinch of lime zest. Eat warm.

MAKES 12 PORTIONS (6 SERVINGS)
MAKE AHEAD: NO

Grilled Apricots with Serrano Ham

Serrano ham—the prosciutto of Spain—is slightly more intense and salty than its Italian cousin and it goes particularly well with fleshy fruits like apricots in the summer or figs in the fall. Look for Serrano ham at specialty food stores and ask for it to be sliced very thinly so you can drape it around the fruit. If unavailable, use prosciutto.

6 large ripe apricots (or 12 fresh figs)

12 paper-thin slices Serrano ham or prosciutto

24 fresh mint leaves

Preheat a broiler and adjust the rack so it is about 4 inches from the heating element.

Cut the apricots into quarters, discarding pits (if using fresh figs, remove the stems and cut figs in half lengthwise). Cut the ham slices in half lengthwise. Drape each apricot quarter (or fig half) with a mint leaf, then wrap a piece of ham over the leaf and around the fruit, pressing gently so it holds. (The apricots or figs can be assembled up to 1 hour ahead, covered, and refrigerated.)

To serve, place the wrapped fruit on a baking sheet and broil until the ham is lightly browned, about 4 minutes. Serve immediately.

MAKES 24 PORTIONS (12 SERVINGS)
MAKE AHEAD: YES

Sausage-Stuffed Cremini

If you think stuffed mushrooms are passé, just watch how quickly these disappear. Cremini are small portobello mushrooms with meaty caps; if you can't find them, use regular white mushrooms.

36 cremini mushrooms
    (about 1½ inch diameter)

Salt

12 ounces mild Italian sausages
    (2 or 3, depending on size)

½ cup packed fresh Italian
    parsley leaves

2 tablespoons fresh oregano leaves
    or 2 teaspoons dried oregano

1 clove garlic

1 slice soft white bread, with crust

½ cup (about 2 ounces) freshly
    grated Parmesan cheese

4 to 6 tablespoons heavy
    (whipping) cream

Freshly ground pepper

Vegetable oil

Preheat the oven to 375 °F.

Wipe the mushrooms clean with a damp paper towel, then twist off the stems to hollow the caps (save stems for another use). Put the mushroom caps in a bowl and sprinkle them well with salt. Toss the mushrooms and salt, then set them aside at room temperature to draw off excess moisture.

Crumble the sausage meat into a large nonstick skillet and cook over medium-high heat, stirring to break up the meat as much as possible. When the sausage is no longer pink, transfer it with a slotted spoon to a paper towel–lined plate to drain.

Put the parsley and oregano in a food processor fitted with the metal blade. With the motor running, drop in the garlic clove and process until finely chopped. Tear the bread into small pieces and add it to the processor; process until the bread is in fine crumbs. Add the drained cooked sausage and pulse until the meat is finely chopped. Transfer the mixture to a bowl and add the cheese; stir well. Pour in 4 tablespoons of the cream and mix well. If the stuffing seems dry, add the remaining cream until the mixture holds together when a small amount is squeezed in your palm. Season to taste with pepper.

Oil a baking sheet. Remove the mushrooms from the bowl and pat off any excess liquid with paper towels. Arrange the caps on a work surface. Spoon the sausage mixture into each cap, mounding it well and packing it with your fingers so it holds firmly, then transfer each cap to the baking sheet. Bake until the stuffing begins to brown on top, 20 to 25 minutes.

Transfer the mushrooms to plates and let them cool for about 10 minutes before serving. (The stuffed mushrooms can be made up to 1 day ahead, cooled, covered, and refrigerated. Reheat in a 325 °F oven until hot through.)

MAKES 36 PORTIONS (18 SERVINGS)
MAKE AHEAD: YES

Fig and Gorgonzola Crostini with Caramelized Onions

These sophisticated little toasts are perfect for summer and fall parties. Guests can't seem to get enough of this combination of sweet onions, ripe figs, and melted Gorgonzola.

Extra-virgin olive oil

1 medium yellow onion, halved and thinly sliced

1 teaspoon sugar

1 teaspoon minced fresh rosemary leaves

Salt

Freshly ground pepper

1 baguette (about 1 pound), cut diagonally into 24 quarter-inch-thick slices

About 18 ripe Black Mission figs

5 ounces Gorgonzola cheese

Rosemary sprigs for garnish (optional)

Warm 3 tablespoons oil in a medium nonstick skillet over medium-high heat. Add the onion and cook, stirring, until limp, about 3 minutes. Sprinkle the sugar over the onions and stir well. Turn the heat down to low and spread out the onions in the pan. Cook until the onions are golden brown, about 15 minutes, stirring once or twice. (Be patient; if you rush it, the onions will burn.) Transfer the onions to a small bowl and stir in the rosemary and salt and pepper to taste. (Onions can be cooked up to 1 hour ahead and left at room temperature.)

Preheat a broiler and adjust the rack so it is about 4 inches from the heating element. Brush both sides of the bread slices with oil and broil, turning once, until they are golden. Keep the broiler on.

Spoon some onions onto each piece of bread, dividing equally. Thinly slice the figs and arrange 3 or 4 slices on each bread slice atop the onions. Thinly slice the Gorgonzola and distribute it evenly over the figs. Return the toasts to the broiler and broil until the cheese has melted. Serve warm, with the rosemary sprigs as garnish (if using).

MAKES 24 PORTIONS (12 SERVINGS)
MAKE AHEAD: ONIONS ONLY

Mystery Tidbits and Hasty Hots

This book wouldn't be complete without the party standard of my youth—mayonnaisey, cheesy, broiled canapés. This is for my mom, Callie's mom, Jan, Barb, and all the great ladies who entertained in the heyday of cocktails.

MYSTERY TIDBITS

One 4½-ounce can chopped olives

1 cup (about 4 ounces) shredded
   sharp Cheddar cheese

⅓ cup Best Foods or Hellmann's
   mayonnaise

3 green onions, including tops,
   minced

24 rye bread cocktail rounds

HASTY HOTS

½ cup (about 2 ounces) freshly
   grated Parmesan cheese

½ cup Best Foods or Hellmann's
   mayonnaise

3 green onions, including tops,
   minced

12 slices white bread

Preheat a broiler and adjust the rack so it is about 4 inches from the heating element.

To make the Mystery Tidbits: Mix the olives, cheese, mayonnaise, and onions in a bowl. Arrange the rye rounds on a baking sheet and broil them until toasted on 1 side. Remove the pan and flip the bread. Use a rubber spatula to spread the untoasted sides evenly with the olive mixture. Return the toasts to the broiler and cook until they are bubbly and browned at the edges, 4 to 5 minutes. Serve warm.

To make the Hasty Hots: Mix the cheese, mayonnaise, and green onions in a bowl. Using a 2-inch round cutter, cut 2 circles from each slice of bread (save leftover bread for croutons or bread crumbs). Arrange the bread circles on a baking sheet and broil until they are toasted on 1 side. Remove the pan and flip the bread. Use a rubber spatula to spread the untoasted sides evenly with the cheese mixture. Return the toasts to the broiler and cook until they are bubbly and browned at the edges, 4 to 5 minutes. Serve warm.

MAKES 24 PORTIONS (12 SERVINGS)
MAKE AHEAD: NO

COOL
FINGER FOODS

BECAUSE THEY DON'T HAVE TO BE RUSHED OUT FROM THE

kitchen, these appetizers can be spread around on platters everywhere: in the living room, the dining room, the patio, the hall. They are people magnets, drawing around them groups who want to munch and hang out at the same time. You can have endless fun thinking up bases for cool appetizers, using leaves, vegetables, eggs, pastry, and wontons to carry satisfying toppings to your mouth. I usually find myself eating more of these than anything else, especially at the end of the night when I'm scarfing leftovers in the kitchen and having a post-party debriefing with a few straggling friends.

Baby Artichokes with Lemon Mayonnaise

My mother often greeted guests with tiny steamed artichokes and lemony dip, a very California welcome. If you can't find really small artichokes, trim six large artichokes and remove the fuzzy chokes, then cut each heart into quarters.

3 lemons

24 small artichokes
  (about 3 inches tall)

LEMON MAYONNAISE
1 large egg yolk or 1 large egg

Salt

¼ cup extra-virgin olive oil

½ cup neutral vegetable oil, such
  as safflower

Cut 2 of the lemons in half and squeeze their juice into a bowl filled with cold water, then drop in the squeezed halves. Set the bowl of lemon water next to your work area. Working with 1 artichoke at a time, tear off the dark green leaves until you reach the tender yellow leaves. With a paring knife, trim the bottoms flat (or, if there is a stem, pare off the tough green fibers and leave stem on) and pare away any tough green patches of leaf, then trim off the green tips about ½ inch from the top. Drop each trimmed artichoke into the bowl of lemon water as it is prepared to prevent discoloring.

Drain the artichokes, place them on a steamer rack in a pan above simmering water, and steam, covered, until a knife slides easily through the base (heart) of the artichoke, about 8 minutes. Transfer the artichokes to a plate and let them cool to room temperature.

To make the mayonnaise: Juice the remaining lemon. In a blender, purée the egg yolk with the lemon juice and a hefty pinch of salt. (If using a food processor, use a whole egg.) With the machine running, gradually pour in the olive oil in a very thin, steady stream. Then slowly pour in the vegetable oil in a thin stream. When all of the oil is incorporated, transfer the mayonnaise to a small bowl and season it to taste with more lemon juice and salt. Serve it with the artichokes alongside. (If made ahead, cover and refrigerate the mayonnaise and artichokes separately for up to 1 day.) Garnish with lemon wedges, if desired.

MAKES 24 PORTIONS (12 SERVINGS)
MAKE AHEAD: YES

Stuffed Eggs Caviar-Style

In my opinion, the best way to eat caviar is straight up, with chopped hard-boiled eggs, minced shallots, and toast points. It's also the most expensive way because caviar lovers tend to go overboard. But if you put the same elements together in a stuffed egg, you can stretch that caviar further. To find American osetra and other great caviars, go to www.tsarnicoulai.com.

12 large, hard-boiled eggs

⅓ cup sour cream

1 small shallot, minced

Salt

1 ounce top-quality caviar

Fresh chervil leaves or Italian parsley for garnish (optional)

Peel the eggs and cut them in half lengthwise.

Scoop out the yolks and put them in a bowl; mash them well with a fork. Add the sour cream and shallots and mix well with a fork; season to taste with salt. With a rubber spatula, scrape the yolk mixture into a lock-top plastic bag and push it into 1 corner of the bag. Snip off the corner and pipe the filling into the whites, mounding it slightly. (Or use a pastry bag fitted with a star tip, or fill eggs with a spoon.) The eggs can be made ahead to this point, covered with plastic wrap, and refrigerated for up to 3 hours.

To serve, arrange the eggs on a serving platter and place a small mound of caviar neatly on top of each filled egg. Garnish with the chervil or parsley (if using).

MAKES 24 PORTIONS (12 SERVINGS)
MAKE AHEAD: YES

Parmesan-Pepper Twists

Every party needs some of these: long, festive cheese straws that can be placed around the room in tall glasses or short vases or narrow baskets (see page 78). That way, guests can nibble on them as they please.

1 sheet (8 ounces) frozen puff pastry

All-purpose flour

1 large egg white

½ cup (about 2 ounces) freshly grated Parmesan cheese

Freshly ground pepper

Preheat the oven to 400°F.

Remove the puff pastry from the package and let it stand at room temperature until pliable (about 30 minutes); unfold it if necessary. Set the pastry sheet on a lightly floured work surface and with a rolling pin, roll it into a 12-by-14-inch rectangle. Beat the egg white with 1 teaspoon of water, then brush it all over the pastry. Sprinkle the cheese evenly over the surface, working all the way to the edges. Grind a generous amount of pepper over the entire surface. Fold 1 short side of the pastry in half over the other, then gently roll with the rolling pin to the edges to fuse the pastry. With a sharp knife, cut into ½-inch-wide strips along the long edge. Twist the strips into spirals and transfer them to baking sheets, pressing the ends onto the pan to minimize unraveling.

Bake until the twists are golden brown, about 12 minutes. Let them cool in the pans, then gently slide a metal spatula under the twists to release them. (If made ahead, store in airtight containers for up to 1 day.)

MAKES 28 PORTIONS (14 SERVINGS)
MAKE AHEAD: YES

Cured Salmon with Pimentón

Chef Daniel Olivella of B-44, a Spanish restaurant in San Francisco, taught me how to make this velvety, super-easy cured salmon. It's best to make this with wild, not farm-raised fish, such as Pacific king salmon when it's in season. You must use *pimentón de la Vera*, which is smoked paprika from Spain, for the right flavor; regular paprika will not work. Look for pimentón in gourmet food stores or order from www.thespanishtable.com.

1½ pounds top-quality fresh salmon fillet, in one piece, skin on

1½ tablespoons kosher salt

1½ tablespoons sugar

1½ teaspoons pimentón (Spanish smoked paprika)

½ small red onion, minced

2 tablespoons brined capers, rinsed

1 lemon, thinly sliced

Sliced rye or pumpernickel bread

Place the fish skin side down in a glass dish just large enough to hold it snugly. In a small bowl or ramekin, stir together the salt, sugar, and pimentón. Sprinkle the mixture evenly over the salmon; cover it with plastic wrap and rest a dinner plate on top to press down lightly. Refrigerate the salmon for 4 days, turning it over once every 12 hours and replacing the plastic wrap and plate.

To serve, rinse off the salt mixture and pat the fish dry. With a very sharp knife, slice the salmon thinly, sliding a knife under the flesh to remove it from the skin (if it seems difficult to slice, cover with plastic wrap and put it in the freezer for 10 minutes).

Arrange the sliced salmon on a serving platter and sprinkle it with the onions and capers. Arrange the lemon slices around the sides and offer the platter with bread.

MAKES 30 PORTIONS (15 SERVINGS)
MAKE AHEAD: YES

Filet Mignon with Horseradish Cream

This is a classic and one that few dressy parties should be without. The meat can be grilled outdoors if it's a summer party, then sliced and served on the toasts right there—guests love the smell of it cooking.

HORSERADISH CREAM

½ cup sour cream

2 tablespoons prepared
  horseradish

Salt

Freshly ground pepper

1 baguette (about 1 pound), cut
  diagonally into 24 quarter-
  inch-thick slices

Extra-virgin olive oil

1½ pounds filet mignon steaks
  (about 3), each about 1 inch thick

1 bunch fresh watercress

To make the horseradish cream: In a small bowl, stir together the sour cream and horseradish and season to taste with salt and pepper. Cover and refrigerate the mixture until ready to use (up to ½ hour).

   Preheat a broiler and adjust the rack so it is about 4 inches from the heating element. Brush both sides of the bread slices with oil and broil, turning once, until they are golden. Keep the broiler on. Season the steaks on both sides with salt and pepper to taste, then broil them until medium-rare, 4 to 6 minutes per side. Remove the steaks and let them stand for at least 5 minutes or up to ½ hour before slicing.

   To serve, slice the meat across the grain into 24 thin slices about the length of the bread pieces. Spread 1 side of each baguette slice thickly with the horseradish cream. Pinch the leaves off the watercress sprigs, place a few leaves on each slice, then top with slices of filet mignon.

MAKES 24 PORTIONS (12 SERVINGS)
MAKE AHEAD: NO

Tuna Poke in Wonton Cups

Poke—a chopped salad of ahi tuna, onions, and soy—is traditionally served at a Hawaiian luau and Island chefs now make it with everything from chopped macadamia nuts to truffle oil. I like it mixed with avocado, then served in crunchy wontons. Make sure the tuna is well chilled when you cut it and the avocado isn't too soft or the whole operation will get mushy. Square wonton wrappers are available in the refrigerated section of most supermarkets.

24 wonton wrappers

2 tablespoons Asian sesame oil, divided

12 ounces sashimi-quality ahi tuna, chilled

2 green onions, including tops, thinly sliced

1 tablespoon soy sauce

1 tablespoon freshly squeezed lime juice

1 teaspoon minced fresh ginger

½ large, firm-ripe Haas avocado

Black sesame seeds

Preheat the oven to 350°F.

    Lay the wonton wrappers on a work surface and, using about 1 tablespoon of the oil, brush 1 side of each. Tuck the wonton wrappers into mini-muffin tins, oiled sides down (work in batches if necessary). Snuggle the wrappers into the cups, pleating as necessary to fit. Bake until the wontons are starting to brown on the bottoms and tips, about 8 minutes. Remove the wontons and let them cool in the tins. Let stand for up to 3 hours.

    With a very sharp knife, cut the tuna into ¼-inch-thick slices. Stack the slices and cut them lengthwise into ¼-inch-thick widths. Cut those crosswise into dice (don't worry if pieces aren't perfectly symmetrical). Put the tuna in a small mixing bowl and add the remaining tablespoon oil, the green onions, soy sauce, lime juice, and ginger. Fold gently to mix. Cut the avocado into fine dice and add it to the bowl with the tuna. Fold it in gently to mix. Spoon the poke into the wonton cups and sprinkle with sesame seeds. Serve immediately.

MAKES 24 PORTIONS (12 SERVINGS)
MAKE AHEAD: WONTON CUPS ONLY

Foie Gras Pâté on Brioche with Fig Jam

This one is for luxurious occasions. Buy the smoothest, purest duck or goose liver pâté you can find at a gourmet shop; avoid ones flavored with truffles.

Preparing the jam is a cinch, but if fresh figs aren't in season, buy top-quality fig or sour cherry preserves. Serve any leftover jam as a condiment with grilled lamb or pork.

FIG JAM
8 ounces (8 to 10) ripe Black Mission figs

½ cup fruity red wine, such as Zinfandel

¼ cup sugar

1 teaspoon grated orange zest

Freshly ground pepper

6 to 8 half-inch-thick slices brioche or challah bread

8 ounces duck or goose live pâté, chilled

To make the fig jam: Wash the figs and pat them dry. Trim off the stems and finely chop the figs by hand or in a food processor fitted with the metal blade. Combine the figs in a medium saucepan with the wine, sugar, orange zest, and several grindings of pepper. Bring the mixture to a boil, then reduce the heat to low and cook, uncovered and stirring often, until the mixture is thick and jammy, about 25 minutes. Transfer the fig jam to a bowl and let it cool. (If made ahead, cover and refrigerate for up to 1 week.)

Preheat the oven to 350°F. Cut the bread slices into 24 rounds with a 1½-inch round cutter (you should get 3 to 4 rounds per slice), discarding the crusts. Place on a baking sheet and bake until lightly toasted, about 5 minutes. Remove from the oven and let toasts stand until cool to the touch. (Store in an airtight container for up to 1 day.)

Remove the pâté from the refrigerator just before serving. Cut it into ¼-inch-thick slices, then use a 1-inch round cutter to cut the pâté into circles to top each piece of toast (or just spread a neat layer of pâté about ¼ inch thick on each piece of toast). With the tip of a knife, dab some fig jam in the center of each portion of pâté.

MAKES 24 PORTIONS (12 SERVINGS)
MAKE AHEAD: YES

Endive with Crab Salad

When sweet Dungeness crab comes into season in my hometown of San Francisco, we pile it on endive spears even for the most casual drinks with friends. This works with crabmeat of any kind, as long as it is super fresh. For extra color, present each spear on a long leaf of Treviso Radicchio.

2 heads Belgian endive

6 ounces best-quality crabmeat

1 tender inner celery stalk, finely diced (about ¼ cup)

2 tablespoons mayonnaise

1 teaspoon freshly squeezed lemon juice

Salt

Radicchio di Treviso leaves or chives

Trim the base off the endives and separate the heads into leaves; rinse the leaves and pat them dry. In a small bowl, mix the crabmeat, celery, mayonnaise, and lemon juice. Season to taste with salt. Spoon the crab mixture onto the bottom third of each endive leaf (about a heaping teaspoon for each). Nestle the leaves inside the larger Radicchio leaves, or criss-cross two 1-inch pieces of chive over the crab, then serve.

MAKES ABOUT 24 PORTIONS (ABOUT 12 SERVINGS)
MAKE AHEAD: NO

Crostoni with Fava Beans and Ricotta Salata

Each spring, antipasti of favas and cheese pop up on menus all over Italy. Usually a young pecorino is used, but that delicate version isn't always available here. Creamy ricotta salata (made from the whey left over after pecorino is made) can be easier to find and works beautifully. In a pinch, use feta. Buy an Italian country loaf such as pugliese for the base; the larger size makes these *crostoni* as opposed to *crostini*.

1 pound fresh fava beans

¼ cup (about 1 ounce) finely diced ricotta salata, pecorino, or crumbled feta cheese

Extra-virgin olive oil

1 teaspoon fresh thyme leaves

Grated zest of 1 lemon

Salt

Freshly ground pepper

Six ½-inch-thick slices crusty Italian bread

Shell the favas and drop them into boiling water for 2 minutes. Drain, then pop the inner bean out of its skin. Gently mix the fava beans, cheese, 2 tablespoons of oil, the thyme, and lemon zest in a bowl. Season to taste with salt and pepper, then set aside at room temperature for up to 1 hour.

Preheat a broiler and adjust the rack so it is about 4 inches from the heating element. Brush both sides of the bread slices with oil and broil, turning once, until they are golden. (If made ahead, let toasted bread stand at room temperature for up to 1 hour.)

To serve, cut the bread slices in half crosswise and top them evenly with the fava mixture. Or, serve the fava mixture in small containers with breads alongside.

MAKES 12 PORTIONS (6 SERVINGS)
MAKE AHEAD: YES

Tomato–Pine Nut Bruschetta

In Italy, bruschetta means a piece of country bread grilled over an open fire, then swabbed with olive oil and rubbed with garlic and possibly tomato. Here, bruschetta has morphed into a catch-all phrase for toasted bread topped with tomatoes and basil. I add goat cheese and pine nuts for a little more interest.

⅓ cup (1½ ounces) pine nuts

1 baguette (about 1 pound), cut diagonally into 24 quarter-inch-thick slices

Extra-virgin olive oil

1 clove garlic

1¼ pounds ripe tomatoes

Handful of fresh basil leaves (about 10)

Salt

5 ounces fresh goat cheese

In a small nonstick skillet, toast the pine nuts over medium-high heat, shaking the pan often, for 3 to 5 minutes or until the nuts are golden brown. Pour the nuts onto a plate and set them aside.

Preheat a broiler and adjust the rack so it is about 4 inches from the heating element. Brush both sides of the bread slices with oil and broil, turning once, until they are golden. Remove the bread from the oven and let it cool slightly, then rub 1 side of each slice with the peeled garlic clove. Set the bread aside.

Core, seed, and finely chop the tomatoes by hand (do not use a food processor as they will get too watery). Stack the basil leaves and cut them in half lengthwise, then slice them crosswise into very fine shreds. Mix the basil with the tomatoes and 2 teaspoons oil in a bowl; season to taste with salt. (The recipe can be made ahead up to this point. Let the nuts, bread, and tomato mixture stand separately at room temperature for up to 4 hours.)

To serve, spread the garlic-rubbed sides of the bread slices with some goat cheese. Spoon the tomato-basil mixture evenly over each slice (first drain off excess juices that might have accumulated if tomatoes were left standing). Sprinkle a few pine nuts over each bruschetta.

MAKES 24 PORTIONS (12 SERVINGS)
MAKE AHEAD: YES

Herbed Goat Cheese with Nasturtiums

I first made this cheese spread on a goat farm in Baja, California, where we ate it rolled into homemade tortillas with nasturtiums picked from the garden. For a dressier look, stuff the mixture right into the peppery flowers (or other edible kinds) from your garden or the farmers' market. Or mound it on endive leaves and garnish with watercress.

Handful of fresh basil leaves (about 10)

1 large green onion, including top

1 clove garlic

2 to 4 tablespoons heavy (whipping) cream

6 ounces fresh goat cheese

About 36 unsprayed fresh nasturtium flowers or 3 heads Belgian endive plus 1 bunch fresh watercress

In a food processor fitted with the metal blade, chop the basil, onion, and garlic with 2 tablespoons of the cream. Crumble in the goat cheese and process until the mixture is smooth, adding 1 or 2 more tablespoons of the cream to get a smooth, spoonable (not thin) consistency. Transfer the mixture to a bowl, cover, and refrigerate until the flavors settle and the cheese firms slightly, at least 1 hour or up to 1 day.

If using nasturtium flowers, dunk them into a bowl of cold water to clean them, drain them on paper towels, and pluck off any long stems. With the tip of a blunt knife, dab about ½ teaspoon of the cheese mixture into the center of each flower and gently push the petals into the cheese mixture so they hug it (you may have extra cheese spread). If using endive, trim the base off each head and separate the heads into leaves; rinse the leaves and pat them dry. Mound about 1 teaspoon of the cheese spread in the bottom third of each leaf and garnish each with a watercress sprig. (Flowers and leaves can be stuffed with cheese spread and refrigerated, covered with plastic wrap, for up to 1 hour before serving.)

MAKES ABOUT 36 PORTIONS (ABOUT 18 SERVINGS)
MAKE AHEAD: YES

Cherry Tomatoes Stuffed with Avocado and Bacon

Use good-sized, classic red cherry tomatoes (which have the sturdiest walls) for this appetizer, not pear-shaped or golden cherry tomatoes. A grapefruit knife makes coring them much easier. To fill the tomatoes, it's quickest to use a pastry bag, but if you don't have one, that grapefruit knife doubles as a filling tool.

24 red cherry tomatoes

3 slices thick-cut bacon

1 large, ripe Haas avocado

1 lemon

Salt

With a sharp paring knife, trim off the stem end of each cherry tomato just enough so that the top is flat. Turn the tomato over and slice off a very small piece of the flesh at the bottom so that the tomato will stand flat. Invert the tomato again and with a grapefruit knife, hollow out the tomato without cutting through the base. Set the tomatoes top down on paper towels to drain.

In a small skillet over medium heat, cook the bacon until crisp. Drain the bacon on a paper towel and set aside to cool.

Mash the avocado in a bowl with the juice of half the lemon. Taste, and add more lemon juice if necessary; season well with salt. With your fingers, crumble 2 strips of the bacon into tiny bits (about the size of bread crumbs) and stir into the avocado. Using a pastry bag fitted with a ½-inch tip, or the tip of the grapefruit knife, fill the tomatoes evenly with the avocado mixture. Crumble the remaining strip of bacon into tiny bits and scatter over the tops of the filled tomatoes. Serve immediately.

MAKES 24 PORTIONS (12 SERVINGS)
MAKE AHEAD: NO

Crostini with Roasted Eggplant, Red Pepper, and Mozzarella

The colors of the Italian flag make an appearance in this rustic antipasto that I first ate years ago in Perugia. There it arrived on large slices of toasted bread (crostoni), but for parties, I spoon it onto small toasts (crostini).

1 medium (about 1 pound) Italian eggplant

Extra-virgin olive oil

1 medium red bell pepper

4 ounces fresh mozzarella cheese

Salt

Freshly ground pepper

1 baguette (about 1 pound), cut diagonally into 24 quarter-inch-thick slices

Handful of fresh basil leaves (about 10)

Preheat a broiler and adjust the rack so it is about 4 inches from the heating element. Cut the eggplant into ½-inch-thick slices. Brush both sides of the slices well with oil, and arrange them in 1 layer on a baking sheet. Broil the slices until they are spotted with brown on top; turn them over and continue to broil until they are spotted with brown on the other side, about 10 minutes total. Transfer the eggplant to a plate to cool.

Cut the red pepper into quarters around the core; discard the stem and seeds. Put the pepper pieces, skin sides up, on a baking sheet and broil them until the skins are charred, about 7 minutes. Transfer the peppers to a plastic bag and close the bag. Leave the broiler on. Let the peppers steam until they are cool to the touch, then pull off the charred skin. Meanwhile, brush both sides of the bread slices with oil and broil, turning once, until they are golden.

Cut the roasted pepper and eggplant into fine dice and combine them in a bowl. Dice the mozzarella and add it to the bowl. Add ¼ cup oil, season to taste with salt and pepper, and mix gently. (If made ahead, cover and let mixture and bread stand separately at room temperature for up to 2 hours.)

To serve, spoon the eggplant-pepper mixture onto the toasted bread. Chop the basil leaves finely and sprinkle over the crostini.

MAKES ABOUT 24 PORTIONS (ABOUT 12 SERVINGS)
MAKE AHEAD: YES

SOMETHING SWEET

drinks, and sparkling company, give them something sweet to remember the evening. Like the tiny candies and pastries that come at the end of a great restaurant meal, each sweet should pack a ton of taste in a small package. You can pass these shortbreads, madeleines, nuts, and truffles on platters as the party is winding down (if people are not headed out to dinner) or set them on a pretty tray or cake stand by the door for guests to pick up on the way out. You can make to-go bags by wrapping a couple of sweets in cellophane and tying them with ribbon, or put them in small gift boxes. It's an unexpected and heartfelt way to say thanks for sharing the evening.

Chocolate-Hazelnut Truffles

I fell in love with chocolate and hazelnuts at school in Italy when I tasted Baci Perugina candies for the first time. Eventually, I created these easy-to-make truffles to capture those flavors. Send off your guests with a few of these and a real kiss to go with them.

1½ cups (6 ounces) hazelnuts

12 ounces top-quality bittersweet chocolate, such as Callebaut, finely chopped

1 cup heavy (whipping) cream

1 tablespoon hazelnut liqueur or vanilla extract

1 tablespoon unsalted butter

About 1 cup unsweetened cocoa powder

Mini-muffin liners or paper candy cups

Preheat the oven to 350°F. Spread the hazelnuts in a pie plate and bake them until they are fragrant, about 12 minutes. Remove the nuts and place them in a large, fine-mesh sieve or colander and rub the nuts with a wadded up clean dish towel until most of the skins slough off. Shake the colander vigorously, then lift out the nuts with a slotted spoon. Chop the nuts finely and set them aside.

In the top of a double boiler or in a metal bowl set over simmering water, combine the chocolate and cream. Cook, stirring with a wooden spoon, until the chocolate is melted and the mixture is smooth. Remove from the heat and stir in the hazelnut liqueur, butter, and hazelnuts. Pour the mixture into a 9-by-13-inch baking dish or other shallow glass pan and let it cool to room temperature, then cover it with plastic wrap and refrigerate until solid (3 hours or preferably overnight).

To make the truffles: Place a large sheet of parchment or waxed paper on a work surface. Sift the cocoa powder onto the paper. Have mini-muffin liners or candy cups alongside. Remove the chocolate mixture from the refrigerator and, working quickly, scoop out a level tablespoon of the mixture and roll it between your palms into a ball. Drop the ball into the cocoa powder, scoot it around gently to coat, then transfer it to a candy cup. Continue with the remaining chocolate mixture (if it gets too soft, return it to the refrigerator to firm up). Your hands will get very chocolaty, so wash and dry them once

(continued)

or twice during the process if necessary. You may also have to sift out more cocoa powder. Refrigerate the truffles until firm before serving. (The truffles can be made ahead, placed in an airtight container, and frozen for up to 1 month. Let them thaw for about 10 minutes before serving; truffles should be eaten cold.)

MAKES ABOUT 40 TRUFFLES (ABOUT 20 SERVINGS)
MAKE AHEAD: YES

Sugar and Spice Walnuts

These shaggy, meringue-like clusters taste of sugar and spice and everything nice. Put handfuls in decorative bags for guests to take home. This recipe makes so many, you might want to bake them at the holidays for gifts.

4 cups (1 pound) shelled walnuts

1 stick (8 tablespoons) unsalted butter

2 large egg whites, at room temperature

Salt

1 cup sugar

1 teaspoon ground cinnamon

1 teaspoon vanilla extract

Preheat the oven to 350°F. Spread the walnuts on a large baking sheet with sides and toast them in the oven until they are fragrant, about 12 minutes. Set aside. In a large roasting pan, melt the butter in the oven. When the butter has melted, remove the pan and let it stand while you prepare the nuts.

In a large bowl, with an electric mixer, beat the egg whites with a pinch of salt until soft peaks form. Beat in the sugar, a little bit at a time, until stiff peaks form, then fold in the cinnamon and vanilla. Fold in the nuts gently. Spread the coated nuts in the roasting pan with the butter, stirring gently. Bake until the nuts are coated with crispy meringue, about 30 minutes. Let them cool in the pan. Once cool, break apart the nuts and serve, or store them airtight for up to 1 week.

MAKES 24 SERVINGS
MAKE AHEAD: YES

Lemon-Ginger Madeleines

These petite, fan-shaped cakes sent Proust into rapture; flavoring them with lemon and ginger has the same effect on me. For best results, buy chunky Australian crystallized ginger and pulse it in a food processor; it's hard to chop it finely enough by hand. Standard madeleine plaques—available in cookware stores—have 12 impressions; ideally, use two pans so that the batter does not have to stand between batches.

1 ⅓ cups all-purpose flour

½ teaspoon baking powder

¼ teaspoon salt

3 large eggs, at room temperature

1 teaspoon vanilla extract

1 teaspoon grated lemon zest

⅔ cup granulated sugar

1 stick (8 tablespoons) unsalted butter, melted and slightly cooled, plus 2 tablespoons for greasing

¼ cup finely chopped crystallized ginger (see headnote)

Powdered sugar for dusting

Preheat the oven to 350 °F. Sift the flour, baking powder, and salt into a bowl. In a mixing bowl with an electric beater, beat the eggs, vanilla, and lemon zest until frothy. Gradually beat in the sugar, then continue beating on high speed for 3 minutes until the eggs are light and thick. Beat in the melted butter. Beat the flour mixture into the egg mixture in 4 additions, scraping the bowl after each addition. Fold in the crystallized ginger.

Brush the madeleine plaques with additional melted butter. Spoon the batter into the plaques, filling each impression about ¾ full. Bake until the madeleines are golden brown along the edges, 12 to 15 minutes, switching the pan positions halfway through. Remove and let the madeleines rest in the pans for 5 minutes, then loosen each one with the tip of a knife and place them ribbed side up on a wire rack set over waxed paper. Let them cool completely, then dust the ribbed sides lightly with powdered sugar. (If made ahead, store the madeleines airtight for up to 2 days and dust them with powdered sugar just before serving.)

MAKES 24 PORTIONS (12 SERVINGS)
MAKE AHEAD: YES

Mocha Shortbread Buttons

There's enough espresso in these cookies to jolt the most serious partyer awake. The shortbreads are small, so plan on four per person.

1 ½ sticks (12 tablespoons) unsalted butter, at room temperature

⅓ cup packed light brown sugar

1 teaspoon vanilla extract

1 ¼ cups all-purpose flour

¼ cup unsweetened cocoa powder

1 tablespoon espresso powder

Pinch of salt

Granulated sugar

In a mixing bowl with an electric beater, beat the butter, brown sugar, and vanilla until fluffy.

In another bowl, sift together the flour, cocoa powder, espresso powder, and salt. Beat the flour mixture into the butter mixture in 4 additions, scraping the bowl after each addition, until the dough is well blended. Scrape the dough onto a piece of parchment paper or waxed paper and divide it in half. Roll each half into a log about 1 inch in diameter and 12 inches long. (If the dough gets too soft to roll, wrap it in plastic wrap and refrigerate it until firmer, about 20 minutes.) Wrap the logs in plastic wrap and refrigerate until very firm, about 1 hour.

To bake, preheat the oven to 350 °F. Line 2 baking sheets with parchment paper. Remove the logs 1 at a time from the refrigerator and cut them into ½-inch-thick slices (24 per log). Arrange the slices on a prepared baking sheet. Repeat with the other log. With the tines of a fork, prick the tops of the shortbreads in 2 neat, parallel rows, then sprinkle them with granulated sugar. Bake until the centers of the shortbreads are just firm, about 15 minutes. Remove them from the oven and tilt the pans toward the counter, gently pulling the parchment paper to slide it onto the counter with the cookies still in place. Let the cookies cool on the paper on the counter. (If made ahead, store the shortbreads airtight for up to 2 days.)

MAKES 48 SHORTBREADS (12 SERVINGS)
MAKE AHEAD: YES

INDEX

TABLE OF EQUIVALENTS

The exact equivalents in the following tables have been rounded for convenience.

LIQUID/DRY MEASURES

U.S.	METRIC
¼ teaspoon	1.25 milliliters
½ teaspoon	2.5 milliliters
1 teaspoon	5 milliliters
1 tablespoon (3 teaspoons)	15 milliliters
1 fluid ounce (2 tablespoons)	30 milliliters
¼ cup	60 milliliters
⅓ cup	80 milliliters
½ cup	120 milliliters
1 cup	240 milliliters
1 pint (2 cups)	480 milliliters
1 quart (4 cups, 32 ounces)	960 milliliters
1 gallon (4 quarts)	3.84 liters
1 ounce (by weight)	28 grams
1 pound	454 grams
2.2 pounds	1 kilogram

OVEN TEMPERATURE

FAHRENHEIT	CELSIUS	GAS
250	120	½
275	140	1
300	150	2
325	160	3
350	180	4
375	190	5
400	200	6
425	220	7
450	230	8
475	240	9
500	260	10

LENGTH

U.S.	METRIC
⅛ inch	3 millimeters
¼ inch	6 millimeters
½ inch	12 millimeters
1 inch	2.5 centimeters